40 Fatal Mistakes to Avoid Wh[...] Your ISMS (ISO 27001)

What the official guides don't tell you... and what could cost you your compliance, your credibility, or your cybersecurity.

Contents

- Writing endless, unreadable policies

- Copy-pasting ISO templates without adapting them

- Neglecting evidence and traceability

- Confusing procedures with forms

- Outsourcing all documentation to a consultant

- Creating too many documents no one will read

- Poor version control

- No agile document management process

- Forgetting the PDCA cycle in your documents

- Not connecting documentation with actual practices

Part 3 – Human & Organizational Mistakes

- Not training teams on the ISMS

- Leaving the ISMS in the hands of a single person

- Excluding business units from the security discussion

- Neglecting internal communication

- Believing "everyone reads the security emails"

- Not addressing cultural resistance

- Turning the ISMS into a control system instead of a tool for improvement

- Forgetting external providers and third parties

- Overprotecting infrastructure but ignoring people

- Failing to recognize security efforts within the organization

Part 4 – Technical, Tooling & Audit Mistakes

- Thinking antivirus replaces risk analysis

- Not linking the ISMS to real incidents

- Overloading tools without coherence

- Not testing continuity and recovery plans

- Confusing technical and organizational measures

- Preparing for the first audit like it's an exam

- Not involving audited teams in the preparation

- Being too defensive with auditor feedback

- Trying to be perfect instead of being honest

- Doing ISO "just to get the stamp," not to improve

Conclusion

Introduction

Why is ISO 27001 still so misunderstood?

Because people still see it as *just* a standard. A formality.
A stamp slapped on an organization to say:

> "We're secure. Everything's protected."

Spoiler: it's not.

ISO 27001 is a powerful tool. But when it's misunderstood, poorly applied, or half-baked, it turns into a **sinkhole for time, budget, and credibility**.

Many ISMS (Information Security Management Systems) are launched with the best intentions...
... only to end up as forgotten PowerPoint slides or untouched ISO documents lost in a drive.

What we often get wrong right from the start:

- Thinking it's purely a technical topic

- Launching without a clear leader (or without top management support)

- Focusing on documentation… and forgetting the reality on the ground

- Applying ISO templates without adapting them

- Training the wrong people — or training too late

This guide is built on real-life experience. Raw. Practical.
Drawn from actual cases in SMEs, large corporations, and public sector organizations.

You'll find 40 mistakes we've seen **way too often** —
and most importantly: **how to avoid them**.

1. Thinking an ISMS is just an IT project

The mistake
"Well, it's about security, so it's an IT thing, right?"
That's one of the worst shortcuts you can take. Reducing the ISMS to a technical topic means missing the real value of ISO 27001 — which is about **governance, organization, and strategic control**.
An ISMS is **not** an IT project. It's a **company-wide framework** for managing information security.

What this leads to

- The CISO ends up isolated, with little influence

- Business teams aren't engaged at all

- Truly sensitive information is never identified

- End result: a disconnected, artificial ISMS… and a useless one

How to avoid it

- Establish from day one that information security is a **business-wide issue**, not just a "tech thing"

- Involve **business stakeholders** (HR, legal, operations, sales, etc.)

- Talk about **risk and business value**, not firewalls and antivirus

2. Launching without executive sponsorship

The mistake
"We'll work quietly and just get top management to approve everything at the end."
Bad idea. Without clear and visible support from leadership, your ISMS will carry no weight.
No priorities, no authority, no decisions. It's seen as "just another project" with no strategic value.

What this leads to

- No legitimacy to enforce rules or actions

- Passive resistance ("we'll deal with it later")

- No resources allocated

- No real steering = no progress

How to avoid it

- Secure a high-level sponsor from day one (CEO, C-level, CFO, etc.)

- Speak their language: risks, compliance, reputation, business continuity

- Get a formal and visible commitment (signed policy, charter, presence in committees, etc.)

3. Not defining the ISMS scope properly (too vague or too broad)

The mistake
"We'll just say the scope is the entire company — that way we're covered."
It's a common mistake, often made "to look thorough." But a scope that's too wide (or too blurry) becomes unmanageable.
A poorly defined scope is a **time bomb** when the audit comes around.

What this leads to

- Too many stakeholders to involve = paralysis

- Inconsistencies in risk assessments, controls, and responsibilities

- Constant confusion about what's actually included

How to avoid it

- Define a realistic, manageable scope that makes sense

- Clearly document what's in, what's out, and why

- Don't be afraid to **start small and expand** gradually

- Have the scope validated early by management and key stakeholders

4. Confusing the security policy with the IT usage charter

The mistake
Too many organizations think the "IT usage charter" covers their entire security strategy.
Wrong reflex. The **charter is for users**. The **policy is for steering the ISMS**.
Two levels, two different purposes.

What this leads to

- A vague or nonexistent vision of security priorities

- No clear direction for ISMS actions

- Audit issues as soon as governance is discussed

How to avoid it

- Write a real **security policy**: short, strategic, and approved by top management

- Clarify the company's **security goals, principles, and commitments**

- Make the policy **a living document**: communicate it, review it annually, connect it to your action plan

- And yes, keep the IT usage charter — but in its rightful place (tool use, user behavior)

5. Not setting measurable objectives

The mistake
You hear it all the time: "We want to strengthen security," "Improve compliance," "Raise awareness."
Okay, but **how do you measure that**?
Without indicators and concrete goals, you're flying blind.
And the idea of continuous improvement becomes… just talk.

What this leads to

- No real tracking of ISMS effectiveness

- No audit evidence of objective reviews

- No visible progress — so little internal recognition

How to avoid it

- Define **SMART objectives** (Specific, Measurable, Achievable, Realistic, Time-bound)

Examples:
- → "80% of incidents resolved within 5 days"
- → "100% of new hires trained on security within 30 days"
- → "Internal audit completed every year"

  - Monitor progress regularly, and adjust based on results and shifting priorities

6. Ignoring business stakes in the ISMS design

The mistake
Some ISMS are built in a bubble. Very "tech," very "compliance"... but completely disconnected from real-world operations.
But an ISMS that doesn't understand the business is doomed to be ineffective.

What this leads to

- Useless or inappropriate controls

- No buy-in from business teams

- Wasted resources protecting assets that aren't strategically important

How to avoid it

- Identify **critical business assets** from day one (core apps, client databases, logistics processes, etc.)

- Involve business teams in **risk analysis**

- Align the ISMS with the company's **strategic goals**: production, reputation, customer trust, profitability

- Remind everyone: **security is a business enabler**, not a constraint

7. Failing to map real risks

The mistake
Too many organizations skip this step or do a "checkbox" risk analysis. Copy-pasted Excel matrices found on Google.
The result? Risks that are out of touch — not the ones that actually matter.

What this leads to

- Security measures that miss the mark

- Wasted resources "protecting for the sake of protecting"

- Zero credibility when an auditor starts digging

How to avoid it

- Start by identifying **sensitive business assets**, then real-world threats

- Work with business teams to understand their **actual pain points and scenarios**

- Evaluate **business impact**, not just "low/medium/high" at random

- Set up a **recurring risk review process** — not a one-time snapshot

8. Applying a rigid approach "by principle"

The mistake
"ISO 27001 says it, so we do it." You know the drill.
Requirements are applied **to the letter**, without adapting to the real context.
The result: heavy, misunderstood procedures that are quickly bypassed.

What this leads to

- Internal pushback ("another useless process?")

- Controls that are ineffective because they don't fit reality

- An ISMS that becomes a burden instead of a lever

How to avoid it

- Remember: **ISO 27001 is meant to be flexible** — it sets a framework, not a one-size-fits-all method

- Adapt measures to the **size, risks, and culture** of your organization

- Be pragmatic: better a **simple, working procedure** than a 20-page doc no one reads

- Have **business users review each deliverable** before validation

9. Forgetting about continuous monitoring

The mistake
"We've set up the controls — we're good."
Nope. In an ISMS, **what isn't measured doesn't exist**. And what isn't monitored… drifts over time.

What this leads to

- Controls become outdated or are bypassed without anyone noticing

- Incidents go undetected — or are detected too late

- No feedback loop to adjust or improve the system

How to avoid it

- Define monitoring indicators from the start (e.g. logs, alerts, audits, field checks)

- Set up **regular technical and organizational reviews**

- Document deviations — and learn from them

- Keep it simple: **monitoring = observe + understand + act**

10. Not planning for ongoing budget

The mistake

We gave It everything to launch the ISMS — now it should run on ito own."

Classic mistake. Without sustainable funding, your system **loses steam and slowly dies**.

What this leads to

- Cancelled trainings, rushed internal audits, outdated tools

- No follow-up or real continuous improvement

- And in 3 years? Re-certification becomes impossible

How to avoid it

- Plan a **multi-year ISMS budget** from the beginning: training, tools, audits, internal time

- Link budget lines to **business goals** (e.g. fewer incidents, client compliance)

- And remind decision-makers: **maintaining an ISMS costs less than fixing a crisis**

Part 2 – Documentation & Procedural Mistakes

11. Writing long, unreadable security policies

The mistake

You open the security policy. 24 pages. 3,000 words. No clear headings. Long-winded sentences.

You close it — just like 99% of people would.

A security policy needs to be **read and understood**, or it's pointless.

What this leads to

- No one reads it

- No one knows what it says

- And therefore, no one follows it

How to avoid it

- Aim for a **short, clear, and engaging policy** (2–3 pages max)

- One idea per paragraph. Use simple words and action verbs

- Bonus: **have someone outside security review it** to test readability

12. Copy-pasting ISO templates without adapting them

The mistake
You find a nice ISO 27001 template pack online. Perfect — everything's already written.
You replace "Company X" with your company name and think you've saved time.
In reality, you've just created an ISMS that **looks like no one and fits nothing**.

What this leads to

- Procedures that don't match how things actually work

- Absurd or unrealistic requirements

- An auditor who'll spot it in three questions

How to avoid it

- Use templates as **inspiration**, not gospel

- Always start with this question: **"How do we really do it here?"**

- Document the actual process, **improve it**, then formalize it

13. Neglecting evidence management

The mistake
You say you run reviews, audits, training sessions. Great.
But you keep **no trace** of any of it.
And when it's time to prove your ISMS is working... you've got nothing.

What this leads to

- Non-conformities during audits

- Doubts about whether actions were actually taken

- Loss of credibility with top management

How to avoid it

- From the start, **identify the evidence expected** for each requirement (sign-in sheets, tickets, reports, emails, etc.)

- Set up a **simple organization system** (shared drive, clear naming, version control)

- Educate teams: **"No evidence = it didn't happen"**

14. Confusing a procedure with a form

The mistake
You want to document a process, so you create a nice-looking form.
Great.
But no one knows **when, why, or how to use it**.
A procedure is **not** just a document. It's a **clear explanation** of who does what, when, and how.

What this leads to

- "Zombie documents" that no one uses

- Inconsistent practices

- Internal or external audits stuck in confusion

How to avoid it

- For each key process, document a **real, structured procedure** (objective, scope, steps, roles)

- Add supporting materials (forms, checklists, etc.) as **attachments**

- And most importantly: **test it with real users**. If it doesn't hold up in the field, it's worthless

15. Outsourcing all documentation to an external consultant

The mistake
"We paid a firm — they'll take care of everything."
Well… not quite. An ISMS built without internal involvement is **DOA** (dead on arrival).
If no one understands it, **no one will apply it**.

What this leads to

- A theoretical system disconnected from reality

- No knowledge transfer

- Dependence on the consultant + internal rejection

How to avoid it

- Yes, **work with a consultant**, but don't fully outsource the process

- Involve internal teams at every step: drafting, reviewing, validating

- Require **clear knowledge transfer**: what's been done, why, and how to use it after delivery

16. Creating too many documents no one will read

The mistake
"We'll document everything — that way we're covered for the audit."
Result: 80 files, 200 pages, 10 folders… and zero readers.
Too much documentation kills usability.
Too many docs = no one reads them.

What this leads to

- Massive time wasted on writing… and maintaining

- Operational staff completely disengaged

- Auditors instantly sensing: "This is way too polished to be real"

How to avoid it

- Only document what's **actually useful** — no more, no less

- Always ask: **Who's going to use this? When? Why?**

- Better to have **10 useful documents** than **100 useless ones**

17. Not managing document versions properly

The mistake
"Wait… you used the old version?"
Classic. Without proper version control, you lose track. Contradictory documents circulate.
No one knows what's up to date. It's chaos.

What this leads to

- Outdated instructions being applied

- Conflicts during audits ("that's not what the procedure says")

- Loss of trust in the ISMS documentation

How to avoid it

- **Version every document**: version number, date, author, change log

- Use **clear naming conventions** (e.g.)

- **Centralize everything** in a single shared space: the official doc lives there — and only there

18. Not planning for agile document management

The mistake
"We revise everything once a year."
Sounds good on paper... but in reality? Way too rigid. Too slow. Too risky.
Business or tech changes **won't wait for next December**.

What this leads to

- Documentation becomes disconnected from reality

- Delays in reacting to new risks or incidents

- A perception that the ISMS is "frozen" and out of sync with the business

How to avoid it

- Set up a process for **regular reviews + on-demand updates**

- Allow process owners to **suggest changes at any time**

- Think in terms of **document lifecycle**: create → validate → distribute → update → archive

19. Forgetting the PDCA cycle in every document

The mistake
The document is written… and that's it.
But ISO 27001 is based on **PDCA everywhere** (Plan – Do – Check – Act).
If your document doesn't show how it evolves, it's incomplete.

What this leads to

- Static documents that are never questioned

- Practices that stagnate

- A common audit finding: "no evidence of review or continuous improvement"

How to avoid it
In every procedure or policy, include a **review and improvement** section:

→ Review frequency

→ Who reviews it

→ Which criteria (quality, effectiveness, relevance)

And most importantly: **actually do it**.
Log the reviews. Note the decisions. Adjust accordingly.

20. Not linking documentation to real-life practices

The mistake
Your documentation looks great. Structured. Polished.

But… it has **nothing to do with what actually happens**.
People don't follow it — and sometimes, they don't even know it exists.

What this leads to

- Non-conformities as soon as an auditor checks reality

- A complete disconnect between theory and practice

- Documentation seen as useless "paperwork"

How to avoid it

- Write each document **based on real-life operations**, not from a desk

- Involve frontline staff in validation

- Run **cross-checks**: what the doc says vs. what's actually done

- Remember: **good documentation reflects real practices — not idealized ones**

Part 3 – Human & Organizational Mistakes

21. Not training teams on the ISMS

The mistake
The ISMS is progressing, documents are done, audits are coming… but the teams?
They've never been trained.
Some don't even know what an ISMS is.
And then you wonder why no one follows the rules?

What this leads to

- Repeated, avoidable human errors

- The feeling that "it's an IT thing"

- Obvious non-conformities during audits ("Wait, we were supposed to do that?")

How to avoid it

- Roll out **role-specific training** (HR, IT, business units, execs)

- Include **security awareness in onboarding** for all new hires

- Make training **continuous**, not a one-time event

- Use varied formats: e-learning, quizzes, micro-workshops, role-playing, etc.

22. Leaving the ISMS in the hands of one person

The mistake
"The CISO's handling it." Sure. But what if they leave? Or burn out?
If everything depends on a single person, your ISMS becomes a **single point of failure**.

What this leads to

- Overload for that one person

- The system collapses as soon as they disengage

- No backup, no shared ownership

How to avoid it

- Build an **ISMS team**, even a small one, with key contacts across departments

- Document **roles, access rights, and processes**

- Plan for a **trained backup** with a real human continuity plan

23. Excluding business teams from the security discussion

The mistake
You build the ISMS between tech and compliance… and completely forget the end users.
Bad move: the real risks and needs are **on the ground**.

What this leads to

- Security measures that don't fit operational reality

- Near-zero adoption

- The ISMS seen as "top-down bureaucracy"

How to avoid it

- Involve business teams **from the start**: risk analysis, procedures, controls

- Create a network of **business security ambassadors**

- **Value their feedback** — they're the ones actually impacted

24. Neglecting internal communication

The mistake
You launch the ISMS, have everyone sign the policy… then go silent.
No updates. No reminders. No follow-up.
And you expect it to stick?

What this leads to

- Total disinterest

- The feeling that "the ISMS is dead"

- A growing disconnect between teams and security

How to avoid it

- Build a **real internal communication strategy**: regular, clear, multichannel

- Create engaging **security moments** (cafés, challenges, visuals)

- Share what's actually happening: wins, avoided incidents, new measures

- The goal: **make the ISMS part of daily life**, not just a document

25. Believing "everyone reads the security emails"

The mistake
You send out a monthly security newsletter and assume everyone is informed.
Spoiler: 80% don't even open it.

What this leads to

- An illusion of communication

- Security instructions not being followed

- Risky behaviors despite "having sent the info"

How to avoid it

- **Vary your channels**: posters, quick video calls, Slack, intranet, etc.

- Be direct: **1 message = 1 action**

- Use **visual, fast, and engaging formats**

- Even better: **replace top-down info with real conversation**

26. Failing to manage cultural resistance

The mistake
"We apply the rules. Period."
Bad strategy. An ISMS isn't just about controls — it's a **cultural shift**.
And every shift brings resistance, especially when it affects habits.

What this leads to

- Silent rejection ("Sure, boss..." but never followed through)

- Creative workarounds

- The ISMS seen as a burdensome constraint

How to avoid it

- Identify **human blockers early** (lack of time, mistrust, "we've always done it this way")

- Work in **support mode**, not command mode

- Highlight **quick wins** and demonstrate real business value

- Frame the ISMS as a **tool for progress**, not a bureaucratic machine

27. Turning the ISMS into a control system instead of a tool for improvement

The mistake
Everything is focused on compliance, sanctions, and surveillance.
And we forget the key point: an ISMS is meant to support **continuous**

improvement.
If people see it as policing, you lose them.

What this leads to

- Fear, withdrawal, silence when issues happen

- No feedback from the field

- Total breakdown of the improvement process

How to avoid it

- Set a clear tone: **security is here to support, not punish**

- Encourage and **value incident reports and non-conformities**

- Show that the ISMS **evolves thanks to users**, not against them

28. Forgetting suppliers and third parties

The mistake
You've done everything right internally… but what about contractors?
Partners? Freelancers? They access your data, systems, and tools — yet
they're not included in your ISMS.

What this leads to

- Vulnerabilities introduced by external parties

- Vague contracts with no security clauses

- No real control over what leaves your organization

How to avoid it

- Map out all **critical third parties**

- Include **security and compliance clauses** in contracts

- Conduct regular reviews: access, services, incidents, etc.

- **Train them too**: security is a collective chain

29. Overprotecting infrastructure but forgetting people

The mistake
Firewalls, MFA, bastions, SIEM... your infrastructure is bulletproof.
But your people? They click on anything.
Technical security alone isn't enough if the human side is ignored.

What this leads to

- Phishing, human error, data leaks, risky behavior

- Users who are stressed — or even hostile toward security

- A false sense of control, while the real risk is… the keyboard

How to avoid it

- Invest **as much in human security as in tech**

- Focus on awareness, behavior, and personal accountability

- Build a **supportive security culture**, not a blaming one

30. Failing to recognize security efforts in the company

The mistake
You work like crazy to structure the ISMS, reduce risks, respond to incidents…
And no one knows. Not even upper management.
Unseen means unrecognized.

What this leads to

- Demotivation in security teams

- Chronic underinvestment

- No internal momentum or buy-in

How to avoid it

- Communicate wins and results ("+30% incidents handled," "0 critical incidents this year")

- **Recognize the people involved**

- Tell the stories behind the numbers — what security enabled, what was avoided

- Help the org understand that **security is also a business asset**

Part 4 – Technical, Tooling & Audit Mistakes

31. Thinking antivirus replaces risk analysis

The mistake
"Don't worry, we have antivirus."
OK. But **what exactly are you protecting? Against what? Why?**
Having a security tool doesn't mean your risks are identified, assessed, and addressed.

What this leads to

- "Cosmetic" security based on tools, not reality

- Huge blind spots (people, third parties, human error, etc.)

- A false sense of protection

How to avoid it

- Start with a **real risk analysis**: what assets, what scenarios, what impact

- Then select tools that **cover those real risks**

- And always remember: **tools support thinking — they don't replace it**

32. Not linking the ISMS to real incidents

The mistake
You handle security incidents separately, with no connection to your ISMS.
No big-picture analysis. No feedback loop.
Just firefighting.

What this leads to

- The same incidents keep happening

- No continuous improvement

- An ISMS that floats next to reality — instead of being rooted in it

How to avoid it

- Document each incident: cause, impact, actions taken

- Link them to **identified risks and existing measures**

- Use incidents as **raw material** to evolve and improve your ISMS

33. Overloading tools without coherence

The mistake
You collect security tools like Pokémon: antivirus, EDR, DLP, SIEM, bastion hosts, etc.

But they don't talk to each other, they're underused, and not adapted to your real context.

What this leads to

- An unmanageable mess of tools

- Alert fatigue and config overload for teams

- Security gaps — even with a heavy tech stack

How to avoid it

- Start from **real needs and risks**, not shiny tools

- Choose tools that are **integrated, compatible, and right-sized**

- Less is more: **efficiency > quantity**

34. Not testing continuity plans

The mistake
You have a BCP, a DRP, neatly stored in a drive.
But they've never been tested. No simulations, no drills.
And when things go wrong… everyone's improvising.

What this leads to

- Lost time and panic during a crisis

- A huge gap between theory and reality

- Plans that are useless when you need them most

How to avoid it

- Run **regular tests** (at least once a year): system outages, cyberattacks, human unavailability, etc.

- Involve all relevant stakeholders (IT, business units, leadership)

- **Improve the plans after each drill** — real lessons learned

35. Confusing technical measures with organizational ones

The mistake
You think one tool = one control.
But many ISO requirements are **organizational**: roles, responsibilities, processes.
It's not just about "installing a tool."

What this leads to

- Non-conformities during audits

- Technical controls with no governance or oversight

- Over-reliance on IT for topics that go far beyond tech

How to avoid it

- For each security control, identify both the **technical and organizational side**

- Example: "access management" = IAM tool + access rules + HR validation

- **Never ignore the human and governance aspect**, even in tech-heavy topics

36. Preparing for the first audit like it's an exam

The mistake
You cram the night before, print all the documents, brief everyone in a panic...
As if the ISO 27001 audit were a high school oral exam.
Bad strategy. **An audit isn't a test — it's a mirror.**

What this leads to

- Unnecessary stress

- A surface-level "patch job" preparation

- No real continuous improvement

How to avoid it

- Prepare for the audit **throughout the year**, not the night before

- Practice with **realistic internal audits**

- See the audit as a **moment of reflection**, not judgment

37. Not involving audited staff in the preparation

The mistake
You prep for the audit solo, without informing the teams involved.
Result: on audit day, they discover they're being interviewed — without having read the procedures or knowing what to say.
And it shows.

What this leads to

- Confused, vague, or incorrect answers

- An audit that quickly goes off track

- A loss of credibility with the auditor

How to avoid it

- **Inform teams well in advance**: who's involved, why, and how to prepare

- Run short info or simulation sessions

- Remind them the audit is **for them too** — it's feedback on their daily work

38. Being too rigid in response to auditor feedback

The mistake
You shut down as soon as the auditor raises a point.
You challenge everything, you want to "win."
Wrong move: the auditor is not your enemy.
They can be a real source of improvement — if you listen.

What this leads to

- Unnecessary tension

- Blocked discussions

- A defensive and closed-off image

How to avoid it

- Welcome feedback with **active listening**

- Distinguish between **real non-conformities** and suggestions for improvement

- Show that you're open to evolving the system — not stuck defending documents

39. Aiming for perfection instead of being honest

The mistake
You want to show a "perfect" ISMS. Everything's in place, no weaknesses, total control.
But auditors aren't fools.
They can tell when it's **too perfect to be real**.

What this leads to

- A loss of credibility

- Gaps that get hidden instead of being addressed

- No useful conversations to drive improvement

How to avoid it

- Acknowledge imperfections, improvement areas, and current priorities

- Show that you're **in control and moving forward** — not faking it

- Remember: **ISO 27001 doesn't expect perfection — it expects control**

40. Doing ISO "just for the badge," not for real progress

The mistake
You just want the certificate. To reassure a client. To use it as a sales argument. Fine.
But if there's no substance behind it, your ISMS is just **a movie set**.
And eventually, people will notice.

What this leads to

- Team demotivation after certification ("So… we're done now?")

- An ISMS that stagnates or slowly dies

- A loss of meaning and engagement internally

How to avoid it

- Position the ISMS as a **driver of progress and resilience**

- Link security actions to **real business issues** (incidents, operations, customer compliance, etc.)

- Focus on **long-term value**, not just the medal

Conclusion

An ISMS isn't a folder neatly stored on a shared drive.
 It's a **living system** — it should breathe with your organization, adapt, evolve, and above all... actually be useful.

Better an **imperfect but alive ISMS**, understood by your teams, applied daily...
 ... than a perfect ISMS on paper that's dead in practice.

You're not doing security to tick boxes.
You're doing security to **protect what matters**: your data, your business, your clients, your reputation, your future.

Thank You.

Thanks for taking the time to read all the way through.
 If this guide helped you **avoid even one mistake**, then it served its purpose.

The goal wasn't to preach or deliver one universal truth —
 but to **share raw, real-world insights**. Practical, honest, sometimes blunt — always with good intent.

Keep challenging your ISMS.
Keep it alive.
And most of all, **don't forget why you're doing this**: to protect what truly matters.

Take care.
And good luck on your infosec journey.